A Simple Systematic Mariology

A Simple Systematic Mariology

Mark G. Boyer

WIPF & STOCK · Eugene, Oregon

A SIMPLE SYSTEMATIC MARIOLOGY

Copyright © 2015 Mark G. Boyer. All rights reserved. Except for brief quotations in critical publications or reviews, no part of this book may be reproduced in any manner without prior written permission from the publisher. Write: Permissions, Wipf and Stock Publishers, 199 W. 8th Ave., Suite 3, Eugene, OR 97401.

Wipf & Stock
An Imprint of Wipf and Stock Publishers
199 W. 8th Ave., Suite 3
Eugene, OR 97401

www.wipfandstock.com

ISBN 13: 978-1-4982-2345-4

Manufactured in the U.S.A.   04/08/2015

Dedicated to all past and present members of the
Rural Parish Workers of Christ the King,
a secular institute of the Archdiocese of St. Louis
in Fertile, Missouri

Contents

Introduction | ix

1 Lord, have mercy | 1
2 Holy | 4
3 Mother | 9
4 Virgin | 17
5 Miscellaneous | 23
6 Queen | 34
7 Conclusion | 42

   Appendix 1
   The Litany of the Blessed Virgin Mary (Litany of Loreto) | 47
   Appendix 2
   Litany of the Blessed Virgin Mary in the "Order of Crowning an Image of the Blessed Virgin Mary" | 51
   Appendix 3
   List of Marian Liturgical Celebrations and Scripture Texts Assigned for Each | 54
   Appendix 4
   The Common of the Blessed Virgin Mary | 58
   Appendix 5
   Prayer of Blessing from the Order for the Blessing of an Image of the Blessed Virgin Mary in the *Book of Blessings* | 61

Bibliography | 63

Introduction

MARY, THE MOTHER OF Jesus, is known in the Church as Our Lady of Grace, Our Lady of Fatima, Our Lady of Mount Carmel, Our Lady of Sorrows, Our Lady of Guadalupe, Our Lady of Lourdes, Our Lady of the Rosary, Our Mother of Perpetual Help, and more. Her various titles describe her various functions within the Church.

Many books on Mariology, the study or doctrine relating to the Virgin Mary, either treat the liturgical aspects or the devotional aspects of the topic. Here, they are brought together in one seamless presentation. The liturgical aspects, which include the solemnities, feasts, memorials, and optional memorials in Masses throughout a liturgical year along with the Scripture texts assigned to those, are joined with the devotional aspects, which include prayers, the rosary, the Litany of the Blessed Virgin Mary (Litany of Loreto), and the Litany of the Blessed Virgin Mary in the "Order of Crowning an Image of the Blessed Virgin Mary," and the "Order for the Blessing of an Image of the Blessed Virgin Mary" in the *Book of Blessings*.

A good Mariology begins with a good Christology, and not vice-versa. Jesus Christ, the only-begotten Son of God eternally, is one-hundred percent God. Jesus Christ, the incarnate son of Mary, is one-hundred percent human. In the one person of Jesus Christ there are two natures, namely, the divine and the human. When Mary conceived the Son of God in her womb, she simultaneously became the mother of God and the mother of the man, Jesus. She

Introduction

is the mother of God because Jesus Christ is God, and she is the mother of man because Jesus, who became incarnate in her womb by the Holy Spirit, took flesh in her own body. "What the Catholic faith believes about Mary is based on what it believes about Christ," states the *Catechism of the Catholic Church*, "and what it teaches about Mary illumines in turn its faith in Christ."[1]

Once the first councils of the Church declared firmly who Jesus Christ was/is—*homoousios*, of the same substance of God and man—then theology began to speculate how Mary had the singular privilege of conceiving and bearing Jesus Christ, true God and true man, into the world. By a singular privilege Mary was prepared by God from the moment of her conception by her parents in the womb of her mother, traditionally known as Anne (and her father, traditionally known as Joachim) with grace to be the mother of the God-man, Jesus Christ. This means that she was saved in light of the salvation that her Son was bringing to the world; the Church refers to this as her Immaculate Conception. And the result of her giving birth to Jesus Christ and her salvation was resurrection from the dead, referred to as her Assumption into heaven.

Out of this Mariology, firmly grounded in and flowing from Christology, there arise the liturgical and devotional aspects of the life of the Church. The Litany of the Blessed Virgin Mary (Litany of Loreto) summarizes the attributes of Mary of Nazareth from both liturgy and devotion. This book looks at those attributes individually and collectively and demonstrates how they are contained in the solemnities, feasts, memorials, and optional memorials of the Blessed Virgin Mary throughout the liturgical year in the Scripture texts. Where applicable, devotionals seeking Mary's intercession are included.

Jesus, son of Mary, and Christ, son of Mary, is mentioned thirty-five times in *The Quran*, Islam's sacred scriptures. Where appropriate I have included these references. Of course, Islam does not consider Jesus Christ to be God, but thinks of him as a great prophet, like Moses, or an apostle, one sent by God to people. *The*

---

1. *Catechism*, par. 487.

Introduction

Quran declares his mother to be immaculate and obedient to God. While Islam's perspective on Mary differs from that of Christianity—and more specifically Roman Catholicism—it is, nevertheless, important to include references to Mary from *The Quran* which demonstrate Islam's high esteem of the mother of Jesus.

In the pages that follow, using the Litany of the Blessed Virgin Mary (Litany of Loreto) as the guide, these chapters follow: 1. Lord, have mercy; 2. Holy; 3. Mother; 4. Virgin; 5. Miscellaneous; 6. Queen; 7. Conclusion. Each chapter will draw upon Scripture texts and devotional materials to present a simple systematic Mariology. The guide through this process will be the Litany of the Blessed Virgin Mary (Litany of Loreto) assisted by the Litany of the Blessed Virgin Mary in the "Order of Crowning an Image of the Blessed Virgin Mary." Both litanies can be found in the appendices of this book.

Using the Book

This book is designed to be used by individuals for private study and prayer and by ministers for study, prayer, and preaching. A four-part exercise is offered for the entries in every chapter.

1. A title is given.
2. The title is followed by a reflection on the invocations of the Blessed Virgin Mary that illustrates the title. Also provided are Scripture texts and devotional prayers that help to illustrate the title. The reflection is designed to present a Mariology that is grounded in Christology.

    When I quote from the Litany of the Blessed Virgin Mary (Litany of Loreto) and the Litany of the Blessed Virgin Mary in the "Order of Crowning an Image of the Blessed Virgin Mary," no footnotes are given. Both litanies can be found in their entirety in the appendix of this book.

    Where appropriate I quote from the *Catechism of the Catholic Church*. The quotations are meant to help contextualize the other material. At the end of a quote from the

Introduction

Catechism, the reference is indicated by the paragraph number in the footnote. Also, as indicate above, where appropriate I quote from *The Quran* to illustrate what Islam's holy book says about Mary. When quoting from both the "Order of Crowning an Image of the Blessed Virgin Mary" and the "Order for the Blessing of an Image of the Blessed Virgin Mary" in the *Book of Blessings*, the reference is indicated by the paragraph number in the footnote.

Throughout the reflections, I use the masculine pronoun for God, LORD, LORD God, etc. I am well aware that God is neither male nor female, but in order to avoid the repetition of nouns over and over again, I employ male pronouns, as they are also used in most biblical translations.

3. The reflection is followed by a question for journaling or personal meditation. The question functions as a guide for personal appropriation of Mariology. People who like to journal may find the question appropriate for that activity.

4. A prayer summarizes the exercise and the chapter.

It is my hope that through study of and prayer with the Blessed Virgin Mary, the reader will come to a deeper knowledge of and a closer relationship with God through the one who gave birth to his Son, Jesus Christ, who is also the Son of Mary.

Mark G. Boyer
Optional Memorial: Our Lady of Lourdes

1

Lord, have mercy

Lord, have mercy. Christ, have mercy.
Lord, have mercy. Christ, hear us.
Christ, graciously hear us.
God the Father of Heaven, have mercy on us.
God the Son, Redeemer of the world, have mercy on us.
God the Holy Spirit, have mercy on us.
Holy Trinity, One God, have mercy on us.

Litany of the Blessed Virgin Mary (Litany of Loreto)

A Simple Systematic Mariology

Reflection: The Litany of the Blessed Virgin Mary (Litany of Loreto), like all other litanies, is addressed to the Trinitarian God—Father, Son, Holy Spirit—imploring mercy. The refrain, "Lord, have mercy," is a plea to God, asking that people do not get what they deserve. Many people think that "Lord, have mercy" seeks forgiveness from the Triune God, but in reality it asks God not to treat them the way they deserve to be treated, namely, as sinners deserving punishment. Likewise, the refrain, "Christ, have mercy," begs the Son of God not to give people what they deserve. It is followed by "Christ, hear us," which further emphasizes the request for mercy.

THUS, THE LITANY BEGINS: Lord, have mercy. Christ, have mercy. Lord, have mercy. Christ, hear us. Christ, graciously hear us. The Litany of the Blessed Virgin Mary in the "Order of Crowning an Image of the Blessed Virgin Mary" begins in a similar way: Lord, have mercy. Lord, have mercy. Christ, have mercy. Christ, have mercy. Lord, have mercy. Lord, have mercy.

After requesting mercy, the litany invokes the Trinitarian persons by name, as does the Nicene Creed or Profession of Faith, continuing to plead for mercy. It should be noted that in Trinitarian theology the Father in heaven is attributed with creation, the Son is attributed with redemption, and the Holy Spirit is attributed with sanctification. Thus, the litany continues: God the Father of Heaven, have mercy on us. God the Son, Redeemer of the world, have mercy on us. God the Holy Spirit, have mercy on us. Holy Trinity, One God, have mercy on us. The only difference in The Litany of the Blessed Virgin Mary in the "Order of Crowning an Image of the Blessed Virgin Mary" is "God our Father in heaven" instead of "God the Father of heaven."

In one grand chorus of praise the litany begins, beseeching that God—Father, Son, and Holy Spirit—do not deal with people as they deserve. Once people have implored God's Trinitarian mercy, then they ask the Blessed Virgin Mary to pray for them. Here it is important to note that people do not pray to Mary as if she were a goddess. People implore Mary to pray for them to

God. The *Catechism* states that Mary is invoked under the titles of "Advocate, Helper, Benefactress, and Mediatrix."[1] Because of her singular role in redemption, Mary is ranked first of all the saints. Because of her rank, she presents the needs of people to God. It is not that people cannot present their own needs to God; Mary lends assistance in this process. The Prayer of Blessing in "Order for the Blessing of an Image of the Blessed Virgin Mary" in the *Book of Blessings* declares that "the blessed Virgin Mary intercedes as Mother" in God's heavenly city.[2] The *Catechism* states that "her prayer cooperates in a unique way with the Father's plan of loving kindness."[3] "In the faith of this humble handmaid, the Gift of God [that is, the Holy Spirit] found the acceptance he had awaited from the beginning of time."[4] The *Catechism* adds that "Mary prays and intercedes in faith . . . ."[5] Thus, in both litanies, Mary is asked to "pray for us."

Journal/Meditation: What does it mean for you to ask God to have mercy on you? For what do you need to implore the Trinity not to give you what you deserve?

Prayer: Holy Trinity, One God, I cry to you: Have mercy on me. Father, who created me, have mercy on me. Jesus, who redeemed me, have mercy on me. Holy Spirit, who fills me with grace, have mercy on me. Hear my prayer and that of the Blessed Virgin Mary in the name of Christ, my Lord, who lives and reigns with you, Father, and the Holy Spirit, in eternal Trinity, forever and ever. Amen.

---

1. *Catechism*, par. 969.
2. *Blessings*, par. 1286.
3. *Catechism*, par. 2617.
4. Ibid.
5. Ibid., par. 2618.

2

Holy

Holy Mary, pray for us.
Holy Mother of God, pray for us.
Holy Virgin of virgins, pray for us.

Litany of the Blessed Virgin Mary (Litany of Loreto)

Reflection: In the Litany of the Blessed Virgin Mary (Litany of Loreto), the Virgin of Nazareth is referred to first as Holy Mary. On May 31, the Church marks the Feast of the Visitation of the Blessed Virgin Mary. In the passage from Luke's Gospel assigned to this feast, Elizabeth utters a beatitude in honor of Mary's visit: "Blessed are you among women, and blessed is the fruit of your womb" (Luke 1:42). This verse is used in the traditional prayer known as the Hail Mary. In the second half of the prayer, the pray-ers, referring to Mary as the Holy Mother of God, state, "Holy Mary, Mother of God, pray for us sinners, now and at the hour of our death." Likewise, in the prayer known as the *Salve Regina* (Hail, Holy Queen), the pray-ers refer to her as the Virgin Mary and the Holy Queen.[1] An antiphon in honor of Mary begins, "Holy Mary, be a help to the helpless, a strength to the fearful, a comfort to the sorrowful," and another antiphon states, "O Holy Mary, most compassionate of the compassionate, and holiest of all the holy, make intercession for us."[2] This last phrase, make intercession for us, echoes the refrain in the litany, namely, pray for us.

ON SEPTEMBER 12, THE Church may observe the Optional Memorial of the Most Holy Name of Mary which venerates the holy and glorious name of the Blessed Virgin Mary, the Mother of God. On January 1, the Solemnity of Mary, the Holy Mother of God, the Church proclaims the ever-Virgin Mary to be the Mother of God's Son and the Mother of the Church. This is echoed in an antiphon which begins, "O Holy Mother of God, who did worthily deserve to conceive him whom the whole world cannot contain."[3] It is also found in an act of consecration to the Blessed Virgin by St. Francis de Sales, which calls her "Most Holy Mary, virgin Mother of God."[4] These titles for Mary flow out of Christology. Once Jesus

---

1. Cf. Callan, *Prayer Book*, 418.
2. Ibid., 416.
3. Ibid.
4. Ibid., 421.

is declared to be one hundred percent God, Mary is rightly called the Mother of God.

The Virgin of Nazareth is referred to as the holy Virgin of virgins on March 25, the Solemnity of the Annunciation of the Lord. In the gospel passage assigned for this day, Mary is referred to by the narrator as "a virgin engaged to a man whose name was Joseph" (Luke 1:27); later in the story, she declares, "I am a virgin" (Luke 1:34). This description is echoed in an antiphon, which begins, "O Holy Mary, Virgin of virgins, Mother and daughter of the King of kings!"[5] It is also echoed in the Litany of the Blessed Virgin Mary in the "Order of Crowning an Image of the Blessed Virgin Mary" when she is invoked as "Chosen daughter of the Father." Likewise in the prayer *Ave, Maris Stella* (Hail, Star of the Sea), Mary is called the "Virgin of all virgins!" in addition to "Virgin Mother."[6] In the Litany of the Blessed Virgin Mary in the "Order of Crowning an Image of the Blessed Virgin Mary" she is invoked as "Most honored of virgins."

Mary's virginity is also honored in *The Quran*. After narrating the annunciation, the writer records Mary asking, "How can I have a son, O Lord, when no man has touched me?" The Lord answers her, "That is how God creates what he wills. When he decrees a thing, he says, 'Be,' and it is" (3:47). Later in *The Quran*, the narrator declares, "Commemorate Mary in the Book" (19:16). A messenger is sent to tell Mary that the Lord was going "to bestow a good son on [her]" (19:19). "'How can I have a son,' she said, 'when no man has touched me, nor am I sinful?'" (19:20). The messenger states, "'Thus will it be. Your Lord said: 'It is easy for Me...'" (19:21).

Holiness indicates a degree of relationship with God. Psalm 99 declares Israel's God, known as the LORD, to be a great king. Twice the psalmist declares, "Holy is he!" (99:3, 5) The psalm concludes with the exhortation, "Extol the LORD our God, ... for the LORD our God is holy" (99:9). Also, in Leviticus, the LORD tells Moses and the Israelites, "[B]e holy, for I am holy" (11:44). Later in

---

5. Ibid., 415.
6. Lasance, *Prayer-Book*, 565.

chapter nineteen, the LORD again speaks to Moses, saying, "Speak to all the congregation of the people of Israel and say to them: You shall be holy, for I the LORD you God am holy" (19:2). This means that people are to relate to God on his terms; the degree of their relationship is the degree of their holiness.

To describe Mary as holy, as the holy Mother of God, and as the holy Virgin of virgins means that she is exalted, a person perfect in goodness and righteousness, a person devoted entirely to God, and a person worthy of veneration. Thus, the Litany of the Blessed Virgin Mary in the "Order of Crowning an Image of the Blessed Virgin Mary" invokes Mary as "Minister of holiness." The Prayer of Blessing in the "Order for the Blessing of an Image of the Blessed Virgin Mary in the *Book of Blessings* calls her "a model of holiness for all [God's] chosen people."[7] In other words, Mary precedes all others in holiness.[8] According to the *Catechism*, "This is why the 'Marian' dimension of the Church precedes the 'Petrine.'"[9] The degree of her relationship with God was one hundred percent. The *Catechism* states, "Mary, the all-holy ever-virgin Mother of God, is the masterwork of the mission of the Son and the Spirit in the fullness of time."[10] In other words, Mary was as holy as any human being could be holy without being God. Thus, her holiness is a model worthy of imitation. "In Mary," states the *Catechism*, "the Holy Spirit fulfills the plan of the Father's loving goodness. With and through the Holy Spirit, the Virgin conceives and gives birth to the Son of God."[11] Mary collaborates with the "whole work her Son was to accomplish."[12] Thus, according to the Litany of the Blessed Virgin Mary in the "Order of Crowning an Image of the Blessed Virgin Mary," she is "Helper of the Redeemer."

---

7. *Blessings*, par 1287.
8. Cf. *Catechism*, par. 773.
9. *Catechism*, par. 773.
10. Ibid., par. 721.
11. Ibid., par. 723.
12. Ibid., par. 973.

Journal/Meditation: What is the degree of your relationship with God, that is, how are you holy?

Prayer: Pray for me to God, holy Mary. As the holy Virgin of virgins, may I find you to be a model of holiness. As the holy Mother of God, lead me to your Son, my Lord Jesus Christ, who lives and reigns with the Father and the Holy Spirit, one God, forever and ever. Amen.

3

Mother

Mother of Christ, pray for us.
Mother of divine grace, pray for us.
Mother most pure, pray for us.
Mother most chaste, pray for us.
Mother inviolate, pray for us.
Mother undefiled, pray for us.
Mother most amiable, pray for us.
Mother most admirable, pray for us.
Mother of good counsel, pray for us.
Mother of our creator, pray for us.
Mother of our Savior, pray for us.

Litany of the Blessed Virgin Mary (Litany of Loreto)
[Mother of the church, pray for us.]

A Simple Systematic Mariology

Reflection: The Litany of the Blessed Virgin Mary (Litany of Loreto) contains eleven descriptions of Mary as mother. Added to these was Mother of the Church by Vatican Council II. The introduction to the "Order for the Blessing of an Image of the Blessed Virgin Mary in the *Book of Blessings* calls her "Christ's Mother, the Mother of the visible image of the invisible God."[1] On January 1, the Solemnity of Mary, the Holy Mother of God, a passage is read from Paul's letter to the Galatians in which the apostle states, "[W]hen the fullness of time had come, God sent his Son, born of a woman . . ." (4:4). That Son is the Christ, the anointed one. That Son of God is also God; thus, Mary is the Mother of Christ and the Mother of God. Through Mary, people received the author of life, the Lord Jesus Christ. The Litany of the Blessed Virgin Mary in the "Order of Crowning an Image of the Blessed Virgin Mary" invokes Mary as "Mother of Christ the King," and "Mother of the Lord." In the Prayer of Blessing in the "Order for the Blessing of an Image of the Blessed Virgin Mary in the *Book of Blessings*, the pray-er declares, "In her flesh she was [Jesus Christ's] Mother, in her person, his disciple, in her love, his servant."[2] Even *The Quran* refers to "the Christ, son of Mary," and Mary as "a woman of truth" (5:75), even though it does not believe that Jesus Christ was God incarnate.

THE OPTIONAL MEMORIAL OF Our Lady of Lourdes on February 11 presents Mary as the mother of divine grace. In the first passage assigned to this memorial from the prophet Isaiah, Mary is compared to the city of Jerusalem, a mother from whom her children "may nurse and be satisfied from her consoling breast; that they my drink deeply with delight from her glorious bosom" (66:10). The LORD declares that his people "shall nurse and be carried on her arm, and dandled on her knees. As a mother comforts her child, so I will comfort you" (66:12de–13ab). In other words, divine grace flows from Mary as milk flows from a woman's breasts. In the other passage assigned to this day, Gabriel greets Mary as the "favored

1. *Blessings*, par. 1279.
2. Ibid., par. 1286.

one" (Luke 1:28), as a person who has "found favor with God" (1:30). As such, Mary is the mother of divine grace. Indeed, the "Hail Mary" prayer begins with these words: "Hail, Mary, full of grace! The Lord is with you...."[3] The Litany of the Blessed Virgin Mary in the "Order of Crowning an Image of the Blessed Virgin Mary" invokes Mary as "Full of grace" and "Advocate of grace." In the Pious Recommendation to the Blessed Virgin Mary prayer, she is addressed as the "treasure house of grace."[4] The *Catechism* states that the Holy Spirit prepared Mary "by his grace."[5] Thus, she, who is full of grace, becomes the mother of divine grace.

She is also the mother most pure. The Church celebrates her purity on the Saturday after the second Sunday after Pentecost with the Memorial of the Immaculate Heart of the Blessed Virgin Mary. In the gospel passage assigned to the day, the narrator of the story about the boy Jesus getting left behind in the Temple in Jerusalem after celebrating Passover states, "His mother treasured all these things in her heart" (2:51). The same gospel periscope (Luke 2:41–52) is proclaimed in the C cycle of texts for the Feast of the Holy Family, the Sunday between Christmas and January 1. In popular devotion, Mary's motherly purity is often described as immaculate. The Prayer to Our Lady of Mt. Carmel begins by addressing Mary as the "all-blessed, immaculate Virgin."[6] Likewise, the Prayer to Our Lady, Help of Christians, begins "Most holy and immaculate Virgin Mary."[7] In "An Act of Consecration to the Most Holy Heart of Mary," the pray-er begins, "O Heart of Mary, ever Virgin! O heart the holiest, the purest, the most perfect...."[8] Thus, in the Litany of the Blessed Virgin Mary (Litany of Loreto), the invocation states, "Mother most pure, pray for us."

Closely associated with purity, but also distinct from it, is the "mother most chaste" attribute of Mary. In *The Quran*, God

---

3. Bauer, *Essential*, 14.
4. Lasance, *Prayer-Book*, 558.
5. *Catechism*, par. 722.
6. Callan, *Prayer Book*, 423.
7. Ibid.
8. Lasance, *Prayer-Book*, 541.

presents examples of believers. The last example given is that of "Mary, daughter of Imran, who guarded her chastity, so that we breathed into her a life from us, and she believed the word of her Lord and his books, and was among the obedient" (66:12). The Church celebrates the Virgin's chasteness on the Feast of the Nativity of the Blessed Virgin Mary on September 8. One of the prayers from the Mass this day declares that the birth of Jesus "consecrated her integrity;"[9] this is an example of how Mariology flows out of Christology. The gospel passage to be proclaimed on this day refers to Mary's chasteness. Matthew's Gospel declares that she, Jesus' mother, was betrothed to Joseph, but before they lived together she was found with child (1:1–16, 18–23). The Litany of the Blessed Virgin Mary (Litany of Loreto) invokes her as "Mother most chaste." The *Catechism* states that it is by a special grace of God that Mary "committed no sin of any kind during her whole earthly life."[10]

The litany continues with "Mother inviolate," indicating that Mary was a virgin before Jesus' birth, during Jesus' birth, and after Jesus' birth. Mary's virginity is "real and perpetual."[11] On November 21, the Church marks the Memorial of the Presentation of the Virgin Mary, celebrating her inviolateness. The assigned passage from the prophet Zechariah quotes the LORD as saying, "I will come and dwell in your midst" (2:11/2:14). The *Alma Redemptoris* (Mother of the Redeemer) prayer contains a verse to be used during the Christmas Season that refers to Mary's inviolateness. The verse states, "After childbirth, O Virgin, you did remain inviolate."[12]

Very close to the invocation "Mother inviolate" is that of "Mother undefiled." The reference here is to Mary's perfection, her freedom from any impurity, her being immaculate. The Litany of the Blessed Virgin Mary in the "Order of Crowning an Image of the Blessed Virgin Mary" calls her the "Fountain of beauty" and the "First fruit of the redemption." In Mary's Song in Luke's Gospel

9. *Roman Missal*, 942.
10. *Catechism*, par. 411.
11. Ibid., par. 499.
12. Lasance, *Prayer-Book*, 567.

(1:46–55), the Mother undefiled sings about God, who "has looked with favor on the lowliness of his servant" Mary (1:48). Also, the undefiled, lowly servant of God, is a model of those who "associate with the lowly" (Rom 12:16) and are declared blessed. The Church uses both of the above descriptions on the Feast of the Visitation of the Blessed Virgin Mary on May 31.

In a prayer to Our Lady of Good Hope, Mary is referred to as the "Mother of Good Hope." The pray-er addresses her saying that she "fills . . . hearts to overflowing with the sweetest consolation and moves [the pray-er] to hope for every blessing from [her]."[13] This prayer best illustrates the "Mother most amiable" invocation in the Litany of the Blessed Virgin Mary (Litany of Loreto). To be amiable is to be friendly, gracious, pleasant, agreeable. On January 1, the Solemnity of the Blessed Virgin Mary, the Mother of God, the gospel passage assigned to the day emphasizes Mary's amiability. The short passage about the shepherds finding Mary, Joseph, and the Christ child in the manger illustrates Mary's friendliness. Also, the narrator concludes, ". . . Mary treasured all these words and pondered them in her heart" (Luke 2:19), a statement that echoes the prayer to Our Lady of Good Hope.

Closely associated in meaning to amiable is the next invocation of the Litany of the Blessed Virgin Mary (Litany of Loreto), namely, "Mother most admirable." A person who is admirable is one who is praiseworthy, reverence-worthy, and affection-worthy. Even *The Quran* portrays God saying, "O Jesus, son of Mary, remember the favors I bestowed on you and your mother, and reinforced you with divine grace that you spoke to men when in the cradle . . ." (5:110). Here, both Jesus and Mary are admirable. The *Catechism* declares that Mary's "spiritual motherhood extends to all men" and women.[14] She is admirable as the "Handmaid of the Lord," according to the Litany of the Blessed Virgin Mary in the "Order of Crowning an Image of the Blessed Virgin Mary."

The next invocation in the Litany of the Blessed Virgin Mary (Litany of Loreto) is "Mother of good counsel," referring to advice,

---

13. Ibid., *Emmanuel*, 279.
14. *Catechism.*, par. 501.

judgment, or conduct. Mary is often called Our Lady of Good Counsel, as in the prayer by the same name which asks the Virgin to be one's guide and counselor on the earth. The pray-er proceeds to tell Mary his or her need and difficulty and seeks guidance, "how to act in [the] matter," and consultation.[15] Good counsel can be found in the wisdom literature of the Hebrew Bible (Old Testament). For example, on the Feast of the Holy Family, Cycle A, a passage from the Book of Sirach is read (3:2–7) which counsels the reader about honoring his or her father and mother.

"Mother of our Creator" is the next invocation in the Litany of the Blessed Virgin Mary (Litany of Loreto). For the Mass during the Day on Christmas, the beginning of John's Gospel is proclaimed. Particularly appropriate are the words describing the Word through whom all things came into being (cf. 1:3). The Word, the Creator, became flesh in the womb of the Virgin Mary. Thus, Mary is invoked as the mother of the Creator. And because the Word, the Creator, is also the Savior, Mary is invoked as "Mother of our Savior" in the Litany of the Blessed Virgin Mary (Litany of Loreto). The gospel proclaimed during the Mass at Midnight on Christmas makes this clear. An angel of the Lord appears to the shepherds and tells them, ". . . I am bringing you good news of great joy for all the people: to you is born this day in the city of David a Savior, who is the Messiah, the Lord" (2:10–11). Thus, Mary is the "Mother of our Savior."

The last invocation, "Mother of the Church," is not found in the Litany of the Blessed Virgin Mary (Litany of Loreto), but it is found in the Litany of the Blessed Virgin Mary in the "Order of Crowning an Image of the Blessed Virgin Mary" in which Mary is invoked as "Untarnished image of the Church" and "Splendor of the Church." Should the Litany of Loreto ever be revised, it will most likely be added. "Mother of Church" was used by Vatican Council II, which took place 1962–65. In the Prayer of Blessing in the "Order for the Blessing of an Image of the Blessed Virgin Mary" in the *Book of Blessings*, these attributes are brought together. The "Lord God . . . chose the blessed Virgin Mary as the Mother and

---

15. Lasance, *Prayer-Book*, 548.

companion of [his] Son, the image and model of [his] Church, the Mother and advocate of . . . all."[16] Likewise, in the introduction to the "Order for the Blessing of an Image of the Blessed Virgin Mary," the minister states that Mary is "the image and the model of the Church, and she is its exemplar."[17] The introduction continues: "In Mary the Church joyously contemplates the image of all that the Church itself desires and hopes wholly to be. The Church recognizes in Mary the model of the path and the practice it must follow to reach complete union with Christ."[18]

On August 5, the Church marks the Dedication of the Basilica of St. Mary Major in Rome. The gospel passage assigned for this optional memorial portrays a woman in the crowd to whom Jesus is speaking delivering a beatitude: "Blessed is the womb that bore you and the breasts that nursed you!" (Luke 11:27) Jesus, in turn, issues his own beatitude, saying, "Blessed rather are those who hear the word of God and obey it!" (11:28) Jesus' mother, Mary, is the epitome of examples of those who hear the word of God and obey it. After Gabriel tells her that she will conceive and give birth to the Son of God, she declares that she is the servant of God. "Let it be with me according to your word," she tells Gabriel (Luke 1:38). That makes Mary the Mother of the Church, that is, the mother of all those who hear the word of God and obey it.

In Mary, states the *Catechism*, the Church is already holy.[19] She is Mother of the Church at its beginnings with the apostles in the Acts of the Apostles (cf. 1:12–14). Her role "in the Church is inseparable from her union with Christ and flows directly from it," states the *Catechism*.[20] She becomes the Church's "model of faith and charity."[21] In Mary, the Church "contemplates what the Church already is in her mystery on her own 'pilgrimage of faith,' and what

16. *Blessings*, par. 1286.
17. Ibid., par. 1279.
18. Ibid.
19. Cf. *Catechism*, par. 829.
20. *Catechism*, par. 964.
21. Ibid., par. 967.

A Simple Systematic Mariology

she will be in the homeland at the end of her journey."[22] The *Catechism* ties together the first invocation—Mother of Christ—and Mother of the Church.[23]

Journal/Meditation: In what specific ways is Mary a mother for you? What adjectives do you use to describe her motherhood?

Prayer: Almighty God, you made the Virgin of Nazareth the mother of your Son and the mother of your church. Pour on me the same divine grace that you lavished upon Mary that I may serve you free from sin all the days of my life. I ask this through my Lord Jesus Christ, who lives and reigns with you and the Holy Spirit, one God, forever and ever. Amen.

---

22. Ibid., par. 972.
23. Cf. Ibid., par. 963.

4

Virgin

Virgin most prudent, pray for us.
Virgin most venerable, pray for us.
Virgin most renowned, pray for us.
Virgin most powerful, pray for us.
Virgin most merciful, pray for us.
Virgin most faithful, pray for us.

Litany of the Blessed Virgin Mary (Litany of Loreto)

A Simple Systematic Mariology

Reflection: Mary is invoked as Virgin six times in the Litany of the Blessed Virgin Mary (Litany of Loreto), and three times in the Litany of the Blessed Virgin Mary in the "Order of Crowning an Image of the Blessed Virgin Mary." First, she is called "Virgin most prudent." One who is prudent exercises good judgment; he or she is shrewd, discreet, and frugal. The Litany of the Blessed Virgin Mary in the "Order of Crowning an Image of the Blessed Virgin Mary" invokes Mary as the "Model of virtue."

THE SCRIPTURE PASSAGE ASSIGNED as the first reading for the Vigil of Christmas Mass from the prophet Isaiah demonstrates prudence. The prophet states, "For Zion's sake I will not keep silent, and for Jerusalem's sake I will not rest, until her vindication shines out like the dawn, and her salvation like a burning torch" (62:1). Written after some of the Jews had begun to return to Jerusalem from Babylonian captivity, the prophet tells the returned, "You shall no more be termed Forsaken, and your land shall no more be termed Desolate; but you shall be called My Delight Is in Her, and your land Married; for the LORD delights in you, and your land shall be married" (62:4). Just as Mary is most prudent, so does the prophet exhort his readers to exercise good judgment in the presence of God, who has saved his people. Also, from the Isaiah passage comes the Marian invocation "Virgin daughter of Zion" in the Litany of the Blessed Virgin Mary in the "Order of Crowning an Image of the Blessed Virgin Mary."

Mary is also invoked as "Virgin most venerable." To be venerable is to command respect because of one's impressive dignity. Indeed, Mary is a virgin most venerable; she is worthy of reverence due to her noble character. This is best seen in a passage from the prophet Isaiah read numerous times during the liturgical year: 7:10–16. While the passage refers to the birth of King Ahaz's son and serves to assure the king of the future of his Davidic line, the author of Matthew's Gospel applies the passage to Jesus: "Look, the young woman is with child and shall bear a son, and shall name him Immanuel" (7:14). Matthew cites the Septuagint, the Greek translation of the Hebrew Bible, which declares the young woman to be a virgin (1:23). Since the name Immanuel, meaning God-is-with-us, is transferred from the sign given to King Ahaz to a sign given to Jewish-Christians by the author of Matthew's Gospel, Jesus becomes Emmanuel, God-with-us incarnate. While Luke does not quote Isaiah, he alludes to it in his narrative of the annunciation (cf. 1:26–38). Thus, Mary is most worthy of reverence due to her noble character; she cooperated with God to give birth to his Son. "By the Holy Spirit's power and her faith," states the *Catechism*, "her virginity became uniquely fruitful."[1]

Mary is also the virgin most renowned, that is, she is famous and celebrated. The Church marks her fame on May 31, the Feast of the Visitation of the Blessed Virgin Mary. One option of a first reading for this feast is from the prophet Zephaniah (3:14–18a). The prophet describes a new era after the Babylonian captivity of the Israelites. He calls upon daughter Zion, that is, Jerusalem, to sing aloud, and he exhorts the people of Israel to shout. "Rejoice and exult with all your heart, O daughter Jerusalem!" writes Zechariah (3:14cd). The Litany of the Blessed Virgin Mary in the "Order of Crowning an Image of the Blessed Virgin Mary" invokes Mary as "Virgin daughter of Zion," and the Prayer of Blessing in the "Order for the Blessing of an Image of the Blessed Virgin Mary" in the *Book of Blessings* refers to her as "the daughter of Zion, who echoed in her heart the longing of the patriarchs and the hopes of Israel."[2] With this passage, the renowned Virgin Mary is compared to Jerusalem over whom God rejoices with gladness, renews with his love, and exults over with loud singing. "In Mary," states the *Catechism*, "the Holy Spirit manifests the Son of the Father, now become the Son of the Virgin."[3]

The fourth invocation in the Litany of the Blessed Virgin Mary (Litany of Loreto) under the title of virgin is "Virgin most powerful." Jesus' unnamed mother in John's Gospel demonstrates her power at a wedding in Cana of Galilee. When the participants run out of wine, Jesus' mother tells him about the embarrassing

---

1. *Catechism*, par. 723.
2. *Blessings*, par. 1286.
3. *Catechism*, par. 724.

situation. Then, she tells the servants, "Do whatever he tells you" (2:5). Mary is unnamed in John's Gospel because she is a sign of the church, the recipient of God's abundance. Jesus turns the water in six stone jars into wine so the wedding party can continue. *The Quran* refers to her as a sign, too. Allah declares, ". . . We made the son of Mary and his mother a sign . . ." (23:50) of true believers. Mary is the virgin most powerful because of her faith in God.

Mary is also the virgin most merciful. In the hymn attributed to her in Luke's Gospel, Mary sings, "[God's] mercy is for those who fear him from generation to generation" (1:50), and "He has helped his servant Israel, in remembrance of his mercy" (1:54). Mary not only sings about God's mercy, but she demonstrates compassion to those to whom she appears, particularly at Guadalupe, Fatima, and Lourdes. The *Salve Regina* (Hail, Holy Queen) prayer/hymn emphasizes her ever-mercifulness when it addresses her as "O clement, O loving, O sweet Virgin Mary."[4] In Luke's Gospel, instead of punishing her wayward Son after he stays behind in Jerusalem, she does not understand what he says to her, but, nevertheless, treasures his words in her heart (cf. 2:41–51). Thus, she demonstrates her mercy.

The final invocation of Mary under the title of virgin is most faithful. The author of Luke's Gospel describes her as "a virgin engaged to a man whose name was Joseph" (1:27); she describes herself as "the servant of the Lord" (1:38) who desires to do his will. Mary is most faithful because she does her duty; she fulfills her promise to God. The *Catechism of the Catholic Church* refers to this as "the obedience of faith,"[5] and the Litany of the Blessed Virgin Mary in the "Order of Crowning an Image of the Blessed Virgin Mary" invokes her as "Virgin gentle and obedient." Mary "gave herself entirely to the person and to the work of her Son; she did so in order to serve the mystery of redemption with him and dependent on him, by God's grace."[6] The Litany of the Blessed Virgin Mary in the "Order of Crowning an Image of the Blessed Virgin

---

4. Lasance, *Prayer-Book*, 570.
5. *Catechism*, par. 494.
6. Ibid.

Mary" refers to her as "Virgin poor and humble." The Prayer of Blessing in the "Order for the Blessing of an Image of the Blessed Virgin Mary" in the *Book of Blessings* declares her to be "the poor and lowly servant, who trusted solely in her Lord."[7] Finally, "Mary is a virgin because her virginity is the sign of her faith . . . and of her undivided gift of herself to God's will."[8]

According to the *Catechism*, "From the first formulations of her faith, the Church has confessed that Jesus was conceived solely by the power of the Holy Spirit in the womb of the Virgin Mary, affirming also the corporeal aspect of this event: Jesus was conceived 'by the Holy Spirit without human seed.'"[9] Thus, Mary is invoked as "Glory of the Holy Spirit" in the Litany of the Blessed Virgin Mary in the "Order of Crowning an Image of the Blessed Virgin Mary." Gradually, the deepening of faith in the virginal motherhood of Mary led the Church "to confess Mary's real and perpetual virginity . . . . And so the liturgy of the Church celebrates Mary as . . . the 'ever-virgin.'"[10] Quoting St. Augustine, the *Catechism* declares, "Mary 'remained a virgin in conceiving her Son, a virgin in giving birth to him, a virgin in carrying him, a virgin in nursing him at her breast, always a virgin.'"[11]

Journal/Meditation: What do you find most worthy of further reflection among the attributes of Mary as Virgin most prudent, venerable, renowned, powerful, merciful, and faithful? In what specific ways does your answer apply to you?

Prayer: Almighty Father of the Virgin Mary, you chose this young woman of Nazareth to be the mother of your Son, my Lord Jesus Christ, and prepared her for the mission she was to have in the world. Fill me with the same prudence, mercy, and faith that you lavished upon her. Grant that I may serve you now

---

7. *Blessings*, par. 1286.
8. *Catechism*, par. 506.
9. Ibid., par. 496.
10. Ibid., par. 499.
11. Ibid., par. 510.

through the same Christ, who lives and reigns with you and the Holy Spirit, one God, forever and ever. Amen.

5

Miscellaneous

Mirror of justice, pray for us.
Seat of wisdom, pray for us.
Cause of our joy, pray for us.
Spiritual vessel, pray for us.
Vessel of honor, pray for us.
Singular vessel of devotion, pray for us.
Mystical rose, pray for us.
Tower of David, pray for us.
Tower of ivory, pray for us.
House of gold, pray for us.
Ark of the covenant, pray for us.
Gate of heaven, pray for us.
Morning star, pray for us.
Health of the sick, pray for us.
Refuge of sinners, pray for us.
Comforter of the afflicted, pray for us.
Help of Christians, pray for us.

The Litany of the Blessed Virgin Mary (Litany of Loreto)

A Simple Systematic Mariology

Reflection: In the miscellaneous titles category of the Litany of the Blessed Virgin Mary (Litany of Loreto), we find seventeen invocations. While most are very distinct, a few do involve the same basic idea; those invocations that fall into the latter category will be treated together in this chapter.

THE FIRST MISCELLANEOUS INVOCATION is "Mirror of justice." A mirror is a reflecting surface. Mary reflects justice, that is, righteousness, conduct, fair treatment. On the Feast of the Visitation of the Blessed Virgin Mary, May 31, Luke's Gospel passage that records Mary's hymn is proclaimed. In her song, Mary sings about God's justice. God "has brought down the powerful from their thrones, and lifted up the lowly; he has filled the hungry with good things, and sent the rich away empty" (1:52–53). Furthermore, on the Memorial of the Immaculate Heart of the Blessed Virgin Mary, observed on the Saturday following the second Sunday after Pentecost, a passage about the "LORD God causing righteousness and praise to spring up before all the nations" is proclaimed (Isaiah 61:11). Another word for righteousness is justice. Mary is the example or mirror of God's justice. Instead of beginning with what is owed an individual, biblical justice begins with what one owes others. That is why Mary sings about all that God has done and then adds, "Surely, from now on all generations will call me blessed" (Luke 1:48cd).

Mary is the "Seat of wisdom." In order to unpack this invocation, the reader must first understand that a chair is a sign of authority in the ancient world (and somewhat in the modern world). When a king, emperor, or leader spoke, he usually did so while seated in a chair. The word "wisdom" indicates deep insight about what is true and right. While it may entail knowledge, wisdom is not the same as knowing facts; it is about the ability to discern truth from the facts. Mary is a wise authority in terms of the spiritual life. The Hebrew Bible (Old Testament) Book of Proverbs personifies wisdom as a woman whom "the LORD created . . . at the beginning of his work" (8:22a) and who "was beside him, like a master worker" (8:30a). In the Book of Sirach, "Wisdom praises herself, and tells of her glory in the midst of her people" (24:1). She states, "... [T]he Creator of all things gave me a command, and my Creator chose the place for my tent. He said, 'Make your dwelling in Jacob, and in Israel receive your inheritance.' Before the ages, in the beginning, he created me, and for all ages I shall not cease to be" (24:8–9). The author of Luke's Gospel twice portrays Mary as a seat of wisdom. After the shepherds visit her child, the narrator tells the reader, "Mary treasured all these words and pondered them in her heart" (2:19), and after finding the boy Jesus in the temple, "His mother treasured all these things in her heart" (2:51). Thus, because she explores the depth of truth with such sagacity, Mary is invoked as "Seat of Wisdom." The *Catechism* declares: "Mary is acclaimed and represented in the liturgy as the 'Seat of Wisdom.'"[1]

The Litany of the Blessed Virgin also calls her the "Cause of our joy." In the Litany of the Blessed Virgin Mary in the "Order of Crowning an Image of the Blessed Virgin Mary," she is invoked as "Joy of Israel." She brings happiness into the world primarily through the birth of her Son. In Luke's narrative about the birth of Jesus, once he is born angels announce to shepherds "good news of great joy for all the people; to [them] is born this day in the city of David a Savior, who is the Messiah, the Lord" (2:10–11). Then, the heavenly host break out in praise of God, saying, "Glory to God in the highest heaven, and on earth peace among those whom he favors!" (2:14) Thus, Mary is the "cause of our joy" at the birth of God's Son.

The litany devotes three invocations to Mary using the word "vessel": spiritual vessel, vessel of honor, singular vessel of devotion. When applied to a person, the word "vessel" means "holder, receiver, and container." Thus, Mary is being understood as the holder, receiver, and container for the Son of God. Through the prophet Zechariah, God tells the Israelite exiles in Babylon, "I will come and dwell in your midst" (2:10/2:14). This passage is recommended on the Optional Memorial of Our Lady of Mount Carmel

---

1. Ibid., par. 721.

on July 16 because it emphasizes the spiritual vessel invocation. In Mary's womb dwells God.

At the Vigil Mass for the Solemnity of the Assumption of the Blessed Virgin Mary, August 15, the passage from Luke's Gospel about a woman in a crowd shouting to Jesus, "Blessed in the womb that bore you and the breasts that nursed you" (11:27), emphasizes the vessel of honor metaphor, as does the passage from Matthew's Gospel read at the Vigil Mass of Christmas which states that Mary "was found to be with child from the Holy Spirit" (1:18). Luke's Gospel also emphasizes Mary as a vessel of honor. Gabriel tells her, "The Holy Spirit will come upon you, and the power of the Most High will overshadow you; therefore the child to be born will be holy; he will be called Son of God" (1:35).

The *Catechism* has a lot to say about Mary as a vessel of honor. First, "the Holy Spirit prepared Mary by his grace."[2] Second, "in Mary, the Holy Spirit fulfills the plan of the Father's loving goodness. With and through the Holy Spirit, the Virgin conceives and gives birth to the Son of God. By the Holy Spirit's power and her faith, her virginity became uniquely fruitful."[3] Third, "in Mary, the Holy Spirit manifests the Son of the Father, now become the Son of the Virgin. She is the burning bush of the definitive theophany."[4] "Finally, through Mary, the Holy Spirit begins to bring men [and women], the objects of God's merciful love, into communion with Christ."[5]

Besides making Mary the vessel of honor, the Holy Spirit also makes her the singular vessel of devotion. God "has looked with favor on the lowliness of his servant," sings Mary in Luke's Gospel. "Surely, from now on all generations will call [Mary] blessed" (Luke 1:48). The Holy Spirit "is sent to sanctify the womb of the Virgin Mary and divinely fecundate it, causing her to conceive the eternal Son of the Father in a humanity drawn from her own,"

---

2. Ibid., par. 722.
3. Ibid., par. 723.
4. Ibid., par. 724.
5. Ibid., par. 725.

states the *Catechism*.⁶ "The Father's only Son, conceived as man in the womb of the Virgin Mary, is 'Christ,' that is to say, anointed by the Holy Spirit, from the beginning of his human existence . . . ."⁷ Thus, Mary is indeed a singular vessel of devotion.

In the Hebrew Bible (Old Testament) love poem called the Song of Songs or the Song of Solomon, the female states, "I am a rose of Sharon" (2:1). And so Mary is invoked as "Mystical rose" in the Litany of the Blessed Virgin Mary (Litany of Loreto). The word "mystical" refers to the realm of the spiritual. It does not mean what cannot be understood, but carries the connotation of being an unexpected event of God. The fifth chaplet in honor of the Immaculate Heart of Mary, Our Lady of Sorrows, also refers to Mary as a mystical rose. It begins, "O Mary, mystical rose, with loving heart burning with the living fire of charity, you did accept us for your children at the foot of the cross . . . ."⁸ Thus, Mary is compared to a rose, whom God chose from all eternity to be the mother of his Son.⁹

The litany invokes Mary as "tower of David" and "tower of ivory." The word "tower" in each of these invocations refers both to Mary as one who towers over others and as a stronghold. She is a tower of David because her husband Joseph is a "son of David" (Matt 1:20), "descended from the house and family of David" (Luke 2:4). Furthermore, as Gabriel tells Mary, the one she will conceive in her womb "will be called the Son of the Most High, and the Lord God will give to him the throne of his ancestor David" (Luke 1:32). For both of the gospel writers, mentioning this fulfills God's promise given to David: "I will raise up your offspring after you, who shall come forth from your body, and I will establish his kingdom" (2 Sam 7:13). Psalm 89 also contains this promise, portraying the LORD saying, "I will establish [David's] line forever, and his throne as long as the heavens endure" (:29). On September 8, the Feast of the Nativity of the Blessed Virgin

---

6. Ibid., par. 485.
7. Ibid., par. 486.
8. Lasance, *Prayer-Book*, 546.
9. Cf. *Catechism*, par. 488.

Mary, a passage from the prophet Micah is proclaimed that refers to David's hometown, Bethlehem. The prophet records the LORD declaring, ". . . [Y]ou, O Bethlehem of Ephrathah, who are one of the little clans of Judah, from you shall come forth for me one who is to rule in Israel, whose origin is from of old, from ancient days" (5:2). Thus, Mary becomes a tower of David.

The invocation "tower of ivory" comes from the Song of Songs or Song of Solomon. The man in the love poem describes the woman's neck as being like "an ivory tower" (7:4a), that is, she is like majestic architecture. In the biblical world, ivory was widely used for ornamentation; the remains of ancient ivory carvings illustrate the fine craftsmanship that existed in the biblical world. Thus, to refer to Mary as a tower of ivory is to praise God's craftsmanship. The *Catechism* explains this, stating, "To become the mother of the Savior, Mary was enriched by God with gifts appropriate to such a role. . . . [I]t was necessary that she be wholly borne by God's grace."[10]

Mary is invoked as "House of gold," a reference to her being a vessel, as noted above, and precious. On August 5, the Optional Memorial of the Dedication of Saint Mary Major in Rome, the first reading compares the Virgin to "the holy city, the new Jerusalem, coming down out of heaven from God, prepared as a bride adorned for her husband" (Rev 21:2). A loud voice announces that "the home of God is among mortals. He will dwell with them" (21:3) in "the city [of] pure gold" (21:18). So, Mary is like a house of gold in whom dwelt a unique holiness which enriched her "from the first instant of her conception."[11]

Borrowing an image from the Hebrew Bible (Old Testament), Mary is invoked as "Ark of the covenant." The ark of the covenant was a small portable box or chest which contained the two tablets of stone upon which were inscribed the commandments. While this image dovetails with the earlier vessel image, Mary is compared to the ark of the covenant in the passage from the First Book of Chronicles assigned to the Vigil Mass for the Solemnity of the

---

10. *Catechism*, par. 490.
11. Ibid., par. 492.

Miscellaneous

Assumption of the Blessed Virgin Mary on August 15. The chronicler explains how "David assembled all Israel in Jerusalem to bring up the ark of the LORD to its place, which he had prepared for it" (15:3). The Levites "brought in the ark of God, and set it inside the tent that David had pitched for it . . ." (16:1). Just as the ark of the covenant was a sign of the presence of Israel's God, the LORD, so is Mary a sign of the presence of God because she carried in her womb, a type of ark, the Son of God, Jesus Christ.

Mary is invoked as "Gate of heaven," which, according to Genesis 3:24 was closed by the LORD God in order "to guard the way to the tree of life." However, later in the same book Jacob has a dream "that there was a ladder set up on the earth the top of it reaching to heaven" (28:12) with the LORD standing beside him and renewing the covenant with him that he had entered into with his grandfather Abraham. After Jacob awakens, he declares, "This is none other than the house of God, and this is the gate of heaven" (28:17). In the prayers *Alma Redemptoris* (Mother of the Redeemer) and *Ave, Maris Stella* (Hail, Star of the Sea), Mary is referred to as the "portal of the sky";[12] in the *Ave Regina Coelorum* (Hail, Queen of Heaven), she is called the "gate of morn, whence the world's true light was born."[13] Mary is invoked as the gate of heaven because God in the person of Jesus Christ came from heaven and took flesh in her womb. Thus, she is like Jacob's ladder connecting heaven and earth.

As the "morning star," Mary is compared to the planet Venus, which is usually the brightest object in the sky; it is the first star to appear at dusk, and it is the last star to disappear at dawn. In praising the high priest, Simon son of Onias, the author of the Old Testament (Apocrypha) Book of Sirach states that he was "like the morning star among the clouds" (50:6a). The author of the Book of Revelation portrays Jesus giving the morning star to the one who conquers (cf. 2:28). However, later in the book Jesus claims that he is "the bright morning star" (22:16) as does 2 Peter 1:19. On the Feast of Our Lady of Guadalupe, December 12, one option

---

12. Collan, *Prayer Book*, 414.
13. Lasance, *Prayer-Book*, 568.

A Simple Systematic Mariology

for a first reading is Revelation 11:19a; 12:1–6a, 10ab, a pieced-together passage that narrates how "a great portent appeared in heaven" (12:1a). The portent is a token, omen, or astrological sign, like that of the morning star. The portent is "a woman clothed with the sun, with the moon under her feet, and on her head a crown of twelve stars" (12:1b). According to the Litany of the Blessed Virgin Mary in the "Order of Crowning an Image of the Blessed Virgin Mary," Mary is the "Woman transformed," the "Woman clothed with the sun," and the "Woman crowned with stars." The woman is the mother of the Messiah, Mary, who, like the morning star, shines brightest of all among humankind. She is the "Pride of the human race," according to the Litany of the Blessed Virgin Mary in the "Order of Crowning an Image of the Blessed Virgin Mary."

Mary is the "health of the sick." The church marks the Optional Memorial of Our Lady of Lourdes on February 11. Lourdes, a market town in southern France, is where the Blessed Virgin Mary appeared eighteen times to Bernadette Soubirous in 1848. Thousands of people make a pilgrimage to the shrine there in order to be lowered into the healing waters. A passage from the prophet Isaiah is recommended for this celebration because in it the LORD declares that "bodies shall flourish like the grass" (66:14b). In the Prayer to Our Lady of Lourdes, Mary is addressed as "health of the sick."[14] In the prayer, Lourdes is declared to be the place where Mary dispenses her favors, where "many sufferers have obtained the cure of their infirmities, both spiritual and corporal...."[15]

In the same prayer, Mary is addressed as the "refuge of sinners,"[16] another of the invocations in the Litany of the Blessed Virgin Mary (Litany of Loreto). In the passage assigned for the Mass during the Day on August 15, the Solemnity of the Assumption of the Blessed Virgin Mary, the author of the Book or Revelation writes about the mother of the Messiah giving birth to a son. Then, he states that she "fled into the wilderness, where she ha[d] a place prepared by God" (12:6), that is, a refuge, a place of shelter or

---

14. Ibid., 561.
15. Ibid.
16. Ibid.

Miscellaneous

safety, a place that protects her from danger. In the litany, she becomes the place of shelter for sinners, interceding on their behalf. In the Pious Recommendation to the Blessed Virgin Mary prayer, she is called the "refuge of us wretched sinners."[17] The *Catechism* makes it very clear that Mary offers protection to those who come to her in their need. "This very special devotion [to Mary in the liturgy of the Church] . . . differs essentially from the adoration which is given to the incarnate Word and equally to the Father and the Holy Spirit . . . ."[18] By Mary's manifold intercession, she continues to bring to people the gifts of eternal salvation.[19] As a refuge of sinners, Mary "in no way obscures or diminishes [the] unique mediation of Christ, but rather shows its power."[20]

In the Prayer to Our Lady of Lourdes, Mary is invoked as "comfort of the afflicted," as she is in the Litany of the Blessed Virgin Mary (Litany of Loreto). This invocation stems from the words of Simeon addressed to her in Luke's Gospel: "a sword will pierce your own soul" (2:35); this passage is read on the Feast of the Holy Family, Cycle B. A reference is made to this verse in the Prayer in Honor of Our Sorrowful Mother: "O Lord, in whose passion, according to the prophecy of Simeon, a sword of sorrow pierced the most sweet soul of Mary, . . . grant . . . that we may call to mind with veneration her transfixion and sufferings."[21] The word "transfixion" in this prayer is a direct reference to the piercing referenced by Simeon.

The last of the miscellaneous invocations is "Help of Christians." In the Litany of the Blessed Virgin Mary in the "Order of Crowning an Image of the Blessed Virgin Mary," she is invoked as "Champion of God's people." Mary is called the "Mother of Perpetual Help" in the Prayer and Consecration to Our Lady of Perpetual Help. She is an advocate, as illustrated in the Novena to Our Lady of Perpetual Help. The pray-er asks her "to obtain . . . the favor" he

---

17. Ibid., 558.
18. *Catechism*, par. 971.
19. Cf. Ibid., par. 969.
20. *Catechism*, par. 970.
21. Lasance, *Prayer-Book*, 542.

or she desires "and the grace to use it for the glory of God."[22] St. Alphonsus, who instituted devotion to Mary under the title of Our Lady of Perpetual Help, is invoked to "beg of her to grant [the petitioner] the favor" he or she is asking "of her power and maternal goodness."[23] The invocation "Help of Christians" is found in the title to the Prayer to Our Lady, Help of Christians. In this prayer, Mary is declared to be the "powerful help of Christians."[24] She is asked to humble enemies, to enlighten the clergy, to preserve the youth, to promote vocations, and to look upon the young, sinners, and the dying. The pray-er asks Mary for help to copy her virtues "so that by word and example [he or she] may, as far as possible in [his or her] state of life, present in the midst of the world a living image of blessed Jesus [her] Son . . . ."[25] Likewise, in the *Angelus* (Angel) Prayer, Mary is asked to pray for the pray-er that he or she "may be made worthy of the promises of Christ."[26] And in the Memorare prayer, the pray-er begins, "Remember, O most gracious Virgin Mary that never was it know that anyone who fled to your protection, implored you help, and sought you intercession, was left unaided," and concludes, "O Mother of the Word Incarnate, despise not my petitions; but in your clemency hear and answer me." Mary can be invoked as the "Help of Christians" because her "role in the Church is inseparable from her union with Christ and flows directly from it."[27]

Journal/Meditation: Which of the miscellaneous invocations is your favorite? What does it disclose to you about Mary?

Prayer: Ever-living God, you have made the Virgin Mary of Nazareth a singular vessel of devotion by conceiving your Son in her womb and making her a new ark of the covenant of your

22. Ibid., 547.
23. Ibid.
24. Callan, *Prayer Book*, 423.
25. Ibid., 423–425.
26. Bauer, *Essential*, 117.
27. *Catechism*, par. 964.

presence. Grant that she may be the health of the sick, the refuge of sinners, and the help of Christians. Hear my prayer in the name of Jesus Christ, the morning star, who lives and reigns with you and the Holy Spirit, one God, forever and ever. Amen.

6

Queen

Queen of Angels, pray for us.
Queen of Patriarchs, pray for us
Queen of Prophets, pray for us.
Queen of Apostles, pray for us.
Queen of Martyrs, pray for us.
Queen of Confessors, pray for us.
Queen of Virgins, pray for us.
Queen of all Saints, pray for us.
Queen conceived without original sin, pray for us.
Queen of the most holy Rosary, pray for us.
Queen of Peace, pray for us.

The Litany of the Blessed Virgin Mary (Litany of Loreto)

Queen

Reflection: In the Litany of the Blessed Virgin Mary (Litany of Loreto), Mary is invoked as queen eleven times. Once Jesus Christ is named king in the Church's liturgy,[1] it is not long before his mother is named queen. The Prayer of Blessing in the "Order for the Blessing of an Image of the Blessed Virgin Mary" in the *Book of Blessings* declares that "the blessed Virgin Mary . . . reigns as Queen" in God's "heavenly city."[2] On August 15, the church marks the Solemnity of the Assumption of the Blessed Virgin Mary. The *Catechism* explains how she was "preserved free from all stain of original sin" so that "when the course of her earthly life was finished," she "was taken up body and soul into heavenly glory, and exalted by the Lord as Queen over all things."[3] The Litany of the Blessed Virgin Mary in the "Order of Crowning an image of the Blessed Virgin Mary" invokes her as "Queen assumed into heaven." On the octave of the Solemnity of the Assumption, the church celebrates the Memorial of the Queenship of the Blessed Virgin Mary (August 22). Psalm 45, a love song addressed to an Israelite king on his wedding day, is one of the Church's favorite responses to honor the queenship of Mary. These verses seem more than appropriate: At the king's right hand "stands the queen in gold of Ophir" (:9b); "Hear, O daughter, consider and incline your ear; forget your people and your father's house, and the king will desire you beauty. Since he is your lord, bow to him; the people of Tyre will seek your favor with gifts, the riches of the people with all kinds of wealth" (:10–13a). The Litany of the Blessed Virgin Mary in the "Order of Crowning an Image of the Blessed Virgin Mary" invokes Mary as "Queen of love."

WHILE THE LITANY OF the Blessed Virgin Mary (Litany of Loreto) does not contain the invocation "queen of heaven," the Litany of the Blessed Virgin Mary in the "Order of Crowning an Image of the Blessed Virgin Mary" does; it adds "Queen of all the earth" and

---

1. Cf. *Roman Missal*, 505–509.
2. *Blessings*, par. 1286.
3. *Catechism*, par. 966.

"Queen of the universe." The *Ave Regina Coelorum* (Hail, Queen of Heaven) begins, "Hail, O Queen of heav'n enthron'd."[4] Likewise, the *Regina Coeli* (Queen of Heaven) begins, "O Queen of heaven, rejoice, Alleluia."[5] The *Salve Regina* (Hail, Holy Queen) begins, "Hail, holy Queen, Mother of mercy;"[6] using another invocation not found in the Litany of the Blessed Virgin Mary (Litany of Loreto), but in the Litany of the Blessed Virgin Mary in the "Order of Crowning an Image of the Blessed Virgin Mary" she is "Queen of mercy."

The first invocation in the litany is "Queen of Angels." Luke's is the only gospel that narrates the event of the angel Gabriel announcing to Mary that she would be the mother of Jesus. It is also the only gospel to record a multitude of angels praising God after Jesus is born. Since angels are the servants and messengers of God to Mary, in giving birth to Jesus, she became the Mother of God and she is invoked as queen of angels.

She is also invoked as queen of patriarchs, such as Abraham, Isaac, Jacob, Joseph, etc., to whom the LORD spoke and appeared. Likewise, Mary is queen of prophets, such as Isaiah, Jeremiah, Ezekiel, Micah, etc., who received God's word and delivered it to his people. Mary is queen of apostles, such as those twelve named in Mark (3:13–19), Matthew (12:15–21), Luke (6:17–19), and Acts (1:13–14); she is mentioned in the Acts of the Apostles as one who was constantly devoting herself to prayer. To these lists must be added Matthias (Acts 1:26), Paul, and Barnabas (Acts 14:14). While the passage does not mention queenship, the unique story in John's Gospel portrays Jesus on the cross entrusting his unnamed mother to the unnamed disciple whom he loved, and entrusting the unnamed disciple to his unnamed mother (cf. 19:25–27); this is the first of two optional gospel passages to be used on September 15, the Memorial of Our Lady of Sorrows. Thus, Mary is queen of patriarchs, prophets, and apostles. The Litany of the Blessed Virgin Mary in the "Order of Crowning an Image of the Blessed Virgin

---

4. Lasance, *Prayer-Book*, 568.
5. Bauer, *Essential*, 118.
6. Lasance, *Prayer-Book*, 570.

Mary" invokes her as "Perfect disciple of Christ." The Church understands that the mission of many holy women in the Hebrew Bible (Old Testament) prepared for Mary's mission in the Christian Bible (New Testament). "After a long period of waiting the times are fulfilled in her, the exalted Daughter of Sion, and the new plan of salvation is established."[7]

Mary is invoked as queen of martyrs. A martyr is a person who willingly suffers death rather than to renounce his or her faith or religion. The author of Luke's Gospel portrays Jesus as a martyr; Pilate (cf. 23:14, 22), Herod (cf. 23:15), a co-crucified criminal (cf. 23:41), and the centurion (cf. 23:47) declare Jesus to be innocent of any crime. Thus, he dies a martyr's death. Using Jesus as a model, Luke presents Stephen as the first Christian martyr in the Acts of the Apostles (cf. 6:1–8:1a). Others follow. The fourth chaplet in Honor of the Immaculate Heart of Mary, Our Lady of Sorrows, addresses Mary as "Glorious Queen of martyrs, whose sacred heart was pierced in her Son's bitter passion by the sword whereof the holy old man Simeon had prophesied."[8] This latter reference to the sword piercing Mary's soul from Luke's Gospel (cf. 2:35) is the second of two optional gospel passage on September 15, the Memorial of Our Lady of Sorrows.

The invocation "Queen of Confessors" refers to those who confess faith in or bear witness to Christ especially during a time of persecution and/or torture but without martyrdom. The title "confessor" is applied to bishops, monks, nuns, ascetics in the wilderness, teachers, etc. In other words, Mary is queen of those who live consistently in a spirit of loving service to God, especially those who bear witness to Christ as effectively as a martyr does by death.

Closely allied with this latter invocation is that of "Queen of Virgins." This invocation refers to countless women who preserved their virginity rather than be married. Many of these virgins are also martyrs, such as St. Lucy, St. Agnes, and Sts. Perpetua and Felicity. Many of these virgins are not martyrs, such as St. Angela

---

7. *Catechism*, par. 489.
8. Lasance, *Prayer-Book*, 545–546.

A Simple Systematic Mariology

Merici, St. Josephine Bakhita, and St. Rose of Lima. Thus, Mary is queen of virgins. The *Catechism* states, "At once virgin and mother, Mary is the symbol and the most perfect realization of the Church . . . ."[9]

The next invocation in the Litany of the Blessed Virgin Mary (Litany of Loreto) names Mary as the "Queen of all Saints."[10] In each of the Three Offerings in Honor of the Blessed Virgin prayer, each invocation begins with these words: "Holiest Virgin, with all my heart I honor you above all the angels and saints." This invocation summarizes all those that have been used before it, namely, queen of angels, patriarchs, prophets, apostles, martyrs, confessors, and virgins. The *Catechism* states that Mary is the Church's model of faith and charity. This makes her a "preeminent and . . . wholly unique member of the Church."[11]

The next invocation describes a doctrine about Mary; she is the "Queen conceived without original sin." This refers to her Immaculate Conception, a Solemnity marked on December 8. The doctrine of the Immaculate Conception was proclaimed by Pope Pius IX in 1854. The *Catechism* records his words: "The most Blessed Virgin Mary was, from the first moment of her conception, by a singular grace and privilege of almighty God and by virtue of the merits of Jesus Christ, Savior of the human race, preserved immune from all stain of original sin."[12] In the gospel text assigned to this celebration, Luke records the angel Gabriel greeting Mary as the "favored one" (1:28), which is often translated as "full of grace." Commenting on this greeting, the *Catechism* states, ". . . [I]n order for Mary to be able to give the free assent of her faith to the announcement of her vocation, it was necessary that she be wholly borne by God's grace."[13] In other words, she "was redeemed from the moment of her conception."[14] She is redeemed "by reason

---

9. *Catechism*, par. 507.
10. Callan, *Prayer Book*, 419–420.
11. *Catechism*, par. 967.
12. Ibid., par. 491.
13. Ibid., par. 490.
14. Ibid., par. 491.

of the merits of her Son."[15] It is by the grace of God that Mary remained free of every personal sin her whole life long.[16]

In one of the texts assigned to the Mass for the celebration of the Immaculate Conception, Mary is understood to be the woman who reverses the enmity between the serpent and Eve. As such, Mary under the title of Our Lady of Grace is depicted as standing on a snake, crushing the head of the serpent. In the first Chaplet in Honor of the Immaculate Heart of Mary, Our Lady of Sorrows, the doctrine of the Immaculate Conception is proclaimed: "Immaculate Virgin, who conceived without sin, did direct every movement of your most pure heart to that God who was ever the object of your love, and who was ever most submissive to his will, obtain for me the grace to hate sin with my whole heart . . . ."[17] Even *The Quran* attests to Mary's Immaculate Conception. An angel tells her, "O Mary, indeed God has favored you and made you immaculate, and chosen you from all the women of the world" (3:42). The *Catechism* declares Mary to be "a mother to us in the order of grace."[18] This motherhood of Mary in the order of grace "continues uninterruptedly from the consent which she loyally gave at the Annunciation and which she sustained without wavering beneath the cross . . . ."[19]

On October 7, the Church celebrates the Memorial of Our Lady of the Rosary. The first reading recommended for Mass this day is a passage from the Acts of the Apostles. Mary is named among other women and the apostles who "were constantly devoting themselves to prayer" (1:14). The rosary is a material object consisting of a string of beads that enables the pray-er to keep track of his or her prayer. The Hail, Holy Queen; the Apostles' Creed; the Lord's Prayer; the Hail Mary; and the Glory Be are prayed in specified sequences while one reflects on one of the four sets of mysteries, especially the last of the Glorious Mysteries: The Crowning of

15. Ibid., par. 492.
16. Cf. Ibid., par. 493.
17. Lasance, *Prayer-Book*, 544–545.
18. *Catechism*, par. 968.
19. Ibid., par. 969.

the Blessed Virgin as Queen of Heaven. This contemplative form of prayer, as it is known today, seems to emerge in the thirteenth century; however, the practice of repeating the same prayer a set number of times most likely existed long before what is known as the rosary came into existence. The Memorial of Our Lady of the Rosary was originally called Our Lady of Victory. In the Prayer to Our Lady of Victory, the "Victorious Lady, . . .who has ever such powerful influence with her divine Son in conquering the hardest of hearts"[20] is asked to intercede for those whom the pray-er is praying. Calling Mary Our Lady of Victory added to her queenship description. In the Litany of the Blessed Virgin Mary in the "Order of Crowning an Image of the Blessed Virgin Mary," Mary is invoked as "Gentle Lady," "Gracious Lady," and "Our Lady."

The last invocation is "Queen of Peace." This invocation is echoed in the hymn, *Ave Maris Stella* (Hail, Star of the Sea). The ever Virgin Mother, by saying yes to Gabriel's request that she bear the Son of God in her womb, "establish[ed] peace below."[21] Luke's Gospel is unique in that it contains hymns that mention peace. Zechariah's canticle states that "the dawn from on high . . . will guide . . . feet into the way of peace" (1:78b, 79c). After Jesus is born, the heavenly host declares "peace on earth among those whom [God] favors" (2:14), which is echoed later by the disciples as Jesus enters Jerusalem triumphantly: "Peace in heaven, and glory in the highest heaven!" (19:38) Finally, aged Simeon begins his canticle of praise, saying, "Master, now you are dismissing your servant in peace, according to your word" (2:29). Calling Mary the queen of peace does not imply the absence of war; it does imply harmony between people and God. And that is what Luke's canticles state.

Invoking the Virgin of Nazareth with the title "queen" eleven times in the Litany of the Blessed Virgin Mary (Litany of Loreto) establishes her as preeminent among the saints and first after the Triune God. She is crowned queen because she gave her consent to God's word, becoming the mother of Jesus. "Espousing the divine will for salvation wholeheartedly, without a single sin to restrain

20. Callan, *Prayer Book*, 426.
21. Ibid., 414.

her, she gave herself entirely to the person and to the work of her Son,"[22] states the *Catechism*. After she was assumed into heaven, he crowned her queen of heaven.

Journal/Meditation: What invocation of Mary as queen most appeals to you? Why?

Prayer: Almighty God, you established your Son as king of the universe through his suffering, death, and resurrection. You established his Virgin Mother as queen of the universe through her obedience to your word. Grant that I may be found worthy to join in the company of angels and saints over whom Mary reigns. Hear my prayer in the name of your Son, Jesus Christ, who lives and reigns with you in the unity of the Holy Spirit, one God, forever and ever. Amen.

---

22. *Catechism*, par. 494.

7

Conclusion

Lamb of God, who takes away the sins of the world,
spare us, O Lord!
Lamb of God, who takes away the sins of the world,
graciously hear us, O Lord!
Lamb of God, who takes away the sins of the world,
have mercy on us.

V. Pray for us, O holy Mother of God.
R. That we may be made worthy of the promises of Christ.

Let us pray.
Grant, we beseech you, O Lord God, that we your servants, may enjoy lasting health of mind and body, and by the glorious intercession of the Blessed Mary, ever Virgin, be delivered from present sorrow and enter into the joy of eternal happiness. Through Christ our Lord. Amen.

(The Litany of the Blessed Virgin Mary (Litany of Loreto)

Conclusion

Reflection: The Litany of the Blessed Virgin Mary (Litany of Loreto) concludes with three invocations to the Lamb of God. In John's Gospel, John the Baptist twice refers to Jesus as the Lamb of God. When John sees Jesus coming toward him, he states, "Here is the Lamb of God who takes away the sin of the world" (1:29). Later, John's Gospel states, "The next day John again was standing with two of his disciples, and as he watched Jesus walk by, he exclaimed, 'Look, here is the Lamb of God!'" (1:35) The Lamb of God reference reaches a crescendo immediately before and after Jesus is crucified. The narrator tells the reader, "Now it was the day of Preparation for the Passover, and it was about noon" (19:14). The reader has to know that noon was when the slaughter of Passover lambs began; this process lasted until shortly before dark. In other words, Jesus dies at the same time as the Passover lambs are being killed; that makes him a new Passover lamb. To confirm this idea, after Jesus dies the narrator tells the reader that Jesus' legs are not broken "so that the scripture might be fulfilled, 'None of his bones shall be broken'" (19:36). While this is a combination of several Hebrew Bible (Old Testament) passages about the preparation of the Passover lamb (cf. Exod 12:10, 12:46; Num 9:12; Ps 34:21), it clearly indicates that Jesus is the new Passover lamb; he will pass over from death to life.

THE THREE INVOCATIONS, "LAMB of God, who takes away the sins of the world," are taken directly from John's Gospel (1:29). All that differs is the responses. The first response, "spare us, O Lord," comes from Mordecai's prayer in the Book of Esther in which he says, "O Lord God and King, . . . spare your people" (C13:15). In other words, it asks Jesus Christ, the Lamb of God, to refrain from harsh treatment, to refrain from harming or destroying sinful people. The second response intensifies the first, begging "graciously hear us, O Lord." The Litany of the Blessed Virgin Mary in the "Order of Crowning an Image of the Blessed Virgin Mary" states "hear us, O Lord." It calls upon Jesus Christ to show kindness and compassion to people. And the third response, "have mercy on us," brings the pray-er back to the beginning of the litany where he or she asked Jesus Christ not to give him or her what he or she deserved as a sinner.

A versicle (abbreviated V.) follows. It illustrates how Mariology flows out of Christology. The Litany of the Blessed Virgin Mary (Litany of Loreto) asks the "holy Mother of God," Mary, to pray for those reciting the litany. The Litany of the Blessed Virgin Mary in the "Order of Crowning an Image of the Blessed Virgin Mary" asks the same of the "glorious mother of the Lord." ". . . [T]he Blessed Virgin is invoked in the Church under the titles of Advocate, Helper, Benefactress, and Mediatrix,"[1] states the *Catechism*. "Mary's function as mother . . . in no way obscures or diminishes [the] unique mediation of Christ, but rather shows its power. . . . [T]he unique mediation of the Redeemer does not exclude but rather gives rise to a manifold cooperation which is but a sharing in this one source."[2]

The response (abbreviated R.) to the versicle, "That we may be made worthy of the promises of Christ"—in the Litany of the Blessed Virgin Mary (Litany of Loreto)—or "That we may become worthy of the promises of Christ"—in the Litany of the Blessed Virgin Mary in the "Order of Crowning an Image of the Blessed Virgin Mary"—further emphasizes Mary's intercession with God. The devotion shown to Mary "differs essentially from the adoration which is given to the incarnate Word and equally to the Father and the Holy Spirit, and greatly fosters this adoration."[3]

The Litany of the Blessed Virgin Mary (Litany of Loreto) concludes with a prayer addressed to God. The pray-ers identify themselves as servants and petition God for health of mind and body. They also ask God to recognize the intercession of Mary so that they may be freed from any present sorrows and one day enter in to the joy of eternal happiness. As always, the prayer is addressed to God through the Lord Jesus Christ. There can be no doubt from

---

1. Ibid., par. 969.
2. Ibid., par. 970.
3. Ibid., par. 971.

Conclusion

the three invocations—Lamb of God—that Jesus Christ not only takes away the sins of the world, but carries all prayer to his Father.

The Litany of the Blessed Virgin Mary in the "Order of Crowning an Image of the Blessed Virgin Mary" concludes with a prayer addressed to the "God of mercy," asking him to "listen to the prayers of [his] servants who have honored [his] handmaid Mary as mother and queen." The prayer requests grace so that the pray-ers may serve God and neighbor and be welcomed into God's kingdom. This request is made through Christ, the Lord.

Journal/Meditation: What do these phrases mean to you: "spare us, O Lord," "graciously hear us, O Lord," and "have mercy on us"?

Prayer: Father, through your Son's death and resurrection, you made him the new Passover lamb, who takes away the sins of the world. Listen to the glorious intercession of his mother, the Blessed Virgin Mary, and keep me, your servant, healthy in mind and body. I ask this in the name of my Lord Jesus Christ, who lives and reigns with you and the Holy Spirit, one God forever and ever. Amen.

Appendix 1

The Litany of the Blessed Virgin Mary (Litany of Loreto)[1]

Lord, have mercy.
Christ, have mercy.
Lord, have mercy.
Christ, hear us.
Christ, graciously hear us.
God the Father of Heaven, have mercy on us.
God the Son, Redeemer of the world, have mercy on us.
God the Holy Spirit, have mercy on us.
Holy Trinity, One God, have mercy on us.
Holy Mary, pray for us.
Holy Mother of God, pray for us.
Holy Virgin of virgins, pray for us.
Mother of Christ, pray for us.
Mother of divine grace, pray for us.
Mother most pure, pray for us.
Mother most chaste, pray for us.
Mother inviolate, pray for us.
Mother undefiled, pray for us.
Mother most amiable, pray for us.
Mother most admirable, pray for us.
Mother of good counsel, pray for us.

---

1. Weller, *Roman Ritual*, 445–450.

Appendix 1

Mother of our Creator, pray for us.
Mother of our Savior, pray for us.
[Mother of the church, pray for us.]
Virgin most prudent, pray for us.
Virgin most venerable, pray for us.
Virgin most renowned, pray for us.
Virgin most powerful, pray for us.
Virgin most merciful, pray for us.
Virgin most faithful, pray for us.
Mirror of justice, pray for us.
Seat of wisdom, pray for us.
Cause of our joy, pray for us.
Spiritual vessel, pray for us.
Vessel of honor, pray for us.
Singular vessel of devotion, pray for us.
Mystical rose, pray for us.
Tower of David, pray for us.
Tower of ivory, pray for us.
House of gold, pray for us.
Ark of the covenant, pray for us.
Gate of heaven, pray for us.
Morning star, pray for us.
Health of the sick, pray for us.
Refuge of sinners, pray for us.
Comforter of the afflicted, pray for us.
Help of Christians, pray for us.
Queen of Angels, pray for us.
Queen of Patriarchs, pray for us.
Queen of Prophets, pray for us.
Queen of Apostles, pray for us.
Queen of Martyrs, pray for us.
Queen of Confessors, pray for us.
Queen of Virgins, pray for us.
Queen of all Saints, pray for us.
Queen conceived without original sin, pray for us.
Queen of the most holy Rosary, pray for us.

The Litany of the Blessed Virgin Mary

Queen of Peace, pray for us.
Lamb of God, who takes away the sins of the world,
spare us, O Lord.
Lamb of God, who takes away the sins of the world,
graciously hear us, O Lord.
Lamb of God, who takes away the sins of the world,
have mercy on us.

V. Pray for us, O holy Mother of God.
R. That we may be made worthy of the promises of Christ.

Let us pray.
    Grant, we beseech you, O Lord God, that we your servants, may enjoy lasting health of mind and body, and by the glorious intercession of the Blessed Mary, ever Virgin, be delivered from present sorrow and enter into the joy of eternal happiness. Through Christ our Lord. Amen.

The above versicle, response, and prayer appear in a slightly different form in *The Roman Ritual* for the Seasons of Lent and Ordinary Time:
    V. Pray for us, God's holy mother.
    R. That we may be made worthy of Christ's promise.

Let us pray.
    Grant us, your servants, O Lord God, we implore, the joy of continual health in body and mind, and by the glorious intercession of the Blessed Mary ever Virgin, free us from present sadness, and establish us in everlasting gladness. Through Christ our Lord. Amen.

During the Season of Advent, the following versicle, response, and prayer are given in *The Roman Ritual*:
    V. The angel of the Lord declared unto Mary.
    R. And she conceived of the Holy Spirit.

Appendix 1

Let us pray.

O God, you did will that at the message of the angel your Word should take flesh in the womb of the Blessed Virgin Mary. So grant that we your humble suppliants, who believe her to be God's mother indeed, may have her as an advocate at your heavenly throne. Through the selfsame Christ our Lord. Amen.

During the Season of Christmas, the following versicle, response, and prayer are given in *The Roman Ritual*:

V. After childbirth you did remain a virgin inviolate.
R. Mother of God, make intercession for us.

Let us pray.

O God, who through the fruitful virginity of Blessed Mary did ensure eternal salvation to the human race, grant, we pray you, that we may experience the intercessory power of her through whom we have been privileged to receive the author of life, Jesus Christ, your Son, our Lord. Amen.

During the Season of Easter, the following versicle, response, and prayer are given in *The Roman Ritual*:

V. Be glad and be joyful, O Virgin Mary, Alleluia!
R. For the Lord is risen verily, Alleluia!

Let us pray.

O God, who through the resurrection of your Son, Christ Jesus, our Lord, did deign to bring joy into the world, grant, we implore you, that through his Virgin Mother, Mary, we may take possession of the bliss of life never ending. Through the same Christ our Lord. Amen.

Appendix 2

Litany of the Blessed Virgin Mary in the "Order of Crowning an Image of the Blessed Virgin Mary"[1]

Lord, have mercy. Lord, have mercy.
Christ, have mercy. Christ, have mercy.
Lord, have mercy. Lord, have mercy.
God our Father in heaven, have mercy on us.
God the Son, Redeemer of the world, have mercy on us.
God the Holy Spirit, have mercy on us.
Holy Trinity, one God, have mercy on us.
Holy Mary, pray for us.
Holy Mother of God, pray for us.
Most honored of virgins, pray for us.
Chosen daughter of the Father, pray for us.
Mother of Christ the King, pray for us.
Glory of the Holy Spirit, pray for us.
Virgin daughter of Zion, pray for us.
Virgin poor and humble, pray for us.
Virgin gentle and obedient, pray for us.
Handmaid of the Lord, pray for us.
Mother of the Lord, pray for us.
Helper of the Redeemer, pray for us.
Full of grace, pray for us.

1. "Crowning," par. 41.

Appendix 2

Fountain of beauty, pray for us.
Model of virtue, pray for us.
Finest fruit of the redemption, pray for us.
Perfect disciple of Christ, pray for us.
Untarnished image of the Church, pray for us.
Woman transformed, pray for us.
Woman clothed with the sun, pray for us.
Woman crowned with stars, pray for us.
Gentle Lady, pray for us.
Gracious Lady, pray for us.
Our Lady, pray for us.
Joy of Israel, pray for us.
Splendor of the Church, pray for us.
Pride of the human race, pray for us.
Advocate of grace, pray for us.
Minister of holiness, pray for us.
Champion of God's people, pray for us.
Queen of love, pray for us.
Queen of mercy, pray for us.
Queen of peace, pray for us.
Queen of angels, pray for us.
Queen of patriarchs and prophets, pray for us.
Queen of apostles and martyrs, pray for us.
Queen of confessors and virgins, pray for us.
Queen of all saints, pray for us.
Queen conceived without original sin, pray for us.
Queen assumed into heaven, pray for us.
Queen of all the earth, pray for us.
Queen of heaven, pray for us.
Queen of the universe, pray for us.
Lamb of God, you take away the sins of the world,
spare us, O Lord.
Lamb of God, you take away the sins of the world, hear us, O Lord.
Lamb of God, you take away the sins of the world,
have mercy on us.

Litany of the Blessed Virgin Mary

V. Pray for us, O glorious Mother of the Lord.
R. That we may become worthy of the promises of Christ.

God of mercy, listen to the prayers of your servants who have honored your handmaid Mary as mother and queen. Grant that by your grace we may serve you and our neighbor on earth and be welcomed into your eternal kingdom. We ask this through Christ our Lord. Amen.

Appendix 3

List of Marian Liturgical Celebrations and Scripture Texts Assigned for Each

January 1: Solemnity of Mary, the Holy Mother of God
Numbers 6:22–27; Psalm 67:2–3, 5–6, 8; Galatians 4:4–7; Luke 2:16–21

Sunday between January 2 and 8: Solemnity of the Epiphany of the Lord
Isaiah 60:1–6; Psalm 72:1–2, 7–8, 10–13; Ephesians 3:2–3a, 5–6; Matthew 2:1–12

February 2: Feast of the Presentation of the Lord
Malachi 3:1–4; Psalm 24:7–10; Hebrews 2:14–18; Luke 2:22–40 or 2:22–32

February 11: Optional Memorial of Our lady of Lourdes
Isaiah 66:10–14c; Judith 13:18bcde–19; John 2:1–11

March 19: Solemnity of St. Joseph, Spouse of the Blessed Virgin Mary
2 Samuel 7:4–5a, 12–14a, 16; Psalm 89:2–5, 27, 29; Matthew 1:16, 18–21, 24a or Luke 2:41–51a

March 25: Solemnity of the Annunciation of the Lord

List of Marian Liturgical Celebrations

Isaiah 7:10–14; 8:10; Psalm 40:7–11; Hebrews 10:4–10; Luke 1:26–38

May 13: Optional Memorial of Our Lady of Fatima
Chosen from the Common of the Blessed Virgin Mary (see Appendix 4)

May 31: Feast of the Visitation of the Blessed Virgin Mary
Zephaniah 3:14–18a or Romans 12:9–16; Isaiah 12:2–3, 4b-6; Luke 1:39–56

Sunday after the second Sunday after Pentecost: Memorial of the Immaculate Heart of the Blessed Virgin Mary
Isaiah 61:9–11; 1 Samuel 2:1, 4–8; Luke 2:41–51

July 16: Optional Memorial of Our Lady of Mount Carmel
Zechariah 2:14–17; Luke 1:46–55; Matthew 12:46–50

July 26: Memorial of Sts. Joachim and Anne, Parents of the Blessed Virgin Mary
Sirach 44:1, 10–15; Psalm 132:11, 13–14, 17–18; Matthew 13:16–17

August 5: Optional Memorial of the Dedication of the Basilica of St. Mary Major
Revelation 21:1–5a; Judith 13:18–20; Luke 11:27–28

August 15: The Solemnity of the Assumption of the Blessed Virgin Mary
Vigil: 1 Chronicles 15:3–4, 15–16; 16:1–2; Psalm 132:6–7, 9–10, 13–14; 1 Corinthians 15:54b–57; Luke 11:27–28
Day: Revelation 11:19a; 12:1–6a, 10ab; Psalm 45:10–12, 16; 1 Corinthians 15:20–27; Luke 1:39–56

August 22: Memorial of the Queenship of the Blessed Virgin Mary
Isaiah 9:1–6; Psalm 113:1–8; Luke 1:26–38

Appendix 3

September 8: Feast of the Nativity of the Blessed Virgin Mary
Micah 5:1–4a or Romans 8:28–30; Psalm 13:6; Matthew 1:1–16, 18–23 or 1:18–23

September 12: Optional Memorial of the Most Holy Name of Mary
Chosen from the Common of the Blessed Virgin Mary (see Appendix 4)

September 15: Memorial of Our Lady of Sorrows
Hebrews 5:7–9; Psalm 31:2–6, 15–16, 20; John 19:25–27 or Luke 2:33–35

October 7: Memorial of Our Lady of the Rosary
Acts 1:12–14; Luke 1:46–55; Luke 1:26–38

November 21: Memorial of the Presentation of the Blessed Virgin Mary
Zechariah 2:14–17; Luke 1:46–55; Matthew 12:46–50

December 8: Solemnity of the Immaculate Conception of the Blessed Virgin Mary
Genesis 3:9–15, 20; Psalm 98:1–4; Ephesians 1:3–6, 11–12; Luke 1:26–38

December 12: Feast of Our Lady of Guadalupe
Zechariah 2:14–17 or Revelation 11:19a; 12:1–6a, 10ab; Judith 13:18–19; Luke 1:26–38 or 1:39–47

December 25: The Solemnity of the Nativity of the Lord (Christmas)
Vigil: Isaiah 62:1–5; Psalm 89:4–5, 16–17, 27, 29; Acts 13:16–17, 22–25; Matthew 1:1–25 or 1:18–25
Midnight: Isaiah 9:1–6; Psalm 96:1–3, 11–13; Titus 2:11–14; Luke 2:1–14
Dawn: Isaiah 62:11–12; Psalm 97:1, 6, 11–12; Titus 3:4–7; Luke 2:15–20

List of Marian Liturgical Celebrations

Day: Isaiah 52:7–10; Psalm 98:1–6; Hebrews 1:1–6; John 1:1–18 or 1:1–5, 9–14

Sunday within the Octave of the Nativity, or, if there is no Sunday, December 30: Feast of the Holy Family of Jesus, Mary, and Joseph

Cycle A: Sirach 3:2–7, 12–14; Psalm 128:1–5; Colossians 3:12–21 or 3:12–17; Matthew 2:13–15, 19–23 or Luke 2:22–40 or 22:22, 39–40 or Luke 2:41–52

Cycle B: Genesis 15:1–6, 21:1–3; Psalm 105:1–6, 8–9; Hebrews 11:8, 11–12, 17–19; Luke 2:22–40 or 2:22, 39–40

Cycle C: 1 Samuel 1:20–22, 24–28; Psalm 84:2–3, 5–6, 9–10; Luke 2:41–52

Appendix 4
The Common of the Blessed Virgin Mary

(When no biblical texts are specified for a Marian celebration or when texts are only suggested, Scripture texts are chosen from the following.)

Reading I from the Old Testament

1. Genesis 3:9–15, 20: God confronts Adam and Eve after they eat forbidden fruit.
2. Genesis 12:1–7: God calls Abraham to go to Canaan.
3. 2 Samuel 7:1–5, 8b–11, 16: God establishes a kingdom for David.
4. 1 Chronicles 15:3–4, 15–16; 16:1–2: David brings the ark of the covenant to Jerusalem.
5. Proverbs 8:22–31: Wisdom is God's craftsman.
6. Sirach 24:1–4, 8–12, 18–21: Wisdom praises God.
7. Isaiah 7:10–14; 8:10: The virgin shall conceive and bear a son.
8. Isaiah 9:1–6: A child is born; a son is given.
9. Isaiah 61:9–11: Rejoice heartily in the LORD.
10. Micah 5:1–4a: Bethlehem-Ephrathah will give birth to a ruler.

The Common of the Blessed Virgin Mary

11. Zechariah 2:14–17: Rejoice, O daughter Zion.

Reading I from the New Testament during the Season of Easter

1. Acts 1:12–14: Mary prays with the apostles.
2. Revelation 11:19a; 12:1–6a, 10ab: A great sign appears in the sky.
3. Revelation 21:1–5a: A new Jerusalem descends from heaven.

Responsorial Psalm

1. 1 Samuel 2:1, 4–8: My heart exults in the LORD.
2. Judith 13:18–19: You are the highest honor of our race.
3. Psalm 45:11–12, 14–17: Listen to me, daughter.
4. Psalm 113:1b–7: Blessed be the name of the Lord.
5. Luke 1:46–55: Mary's song.

Reading II from the New Testament

1. Romans 5:12, 17–19: There is an abundance of grace.
2. Romans 8:28–30: Those God foreknew he also predestined.
3. Galatians 4:4–7: God sent his son, born of a woman.
4. Ephesians 1:3–6, 11–12: God chose us in Christ, before the world began.

Gospel

1. Matthew 1:1–16, 18–23 or 1:18–23: A genealogy of Jesus Christ.

Appendix 4

2. Matthew 2:13–15, 19–23: Joseph and Mary flee to Egypt with Jesus.
3. Matthew 12:46–50: Jesus declares his disciples to be his mother and brothers.
4. Luke 1:26–38: Gabriel tells Mary she will conceive in her womb and bear a son.
5. Luke 1:39–47: Mary visits Elizabeth.
6. Luke 2:1–14: Mary gives birth to Jesus.
7. Luke 2:15b–19: Shepherds find Mary, Joseph, and Jesus in the manger.
8. Luke 2:27–35: Simeon blesses God when Jesus is presented in the Temple.
9. Luke 2:41–52: Mary and Joseph find the twelve-year-old Jesus in the Temple.
10. Luke 11:27–28: Blessed is the womb that carried Jesus.
11. John 2:1–11: The mother of Jesus attends a wedding.
12. John 19:25–27: Jesus entrusts his mother to the beloved disciple, and vice-versa.

Appendix 5

Prayer of Blessing from the Order for the Blessing of an Image of the Blessed Virgin Mary in the *Book of Blessings*[1]

Lord God, we acknowledge your infinite glory and the abundance of your gifts. Before the foundation of the world, your appointed Christ the beginning and end of all things.

You chose the blessed Virgin Mary as the Mother and companion of your Son, the image and model of your Church, the Mother and advocate of us all.

She is the new Eve, through whom you restored what the first Eve had lost. She is the daughter of Zion, who echoed in her heart the longings of the patriarchs and the hopes of Israel.

She is the poor and lowly servant, who trusted solely in her Lord.

In the fullness of time she was delivered of the Sun of justice, the dayspring from on high, your Son, Jesus Christ.

In her flesh she was his Mother, in her person, his disciple, in her love, his servant.

Father, may your children who have provided this image (statue) of Mary know her protection and trace in their hearts the pattern of her holiness.

---

1. *Blessings*, par. 1286–1287.

Appendix 5

Bless them with faith and hope, love and humility; bless them with strength in hardship and self-respect in poverty; bless them with patience in adversity and kindheartedness in times of plenty.

May they search for peace, strive for justice, and realize your love, as they pursue their journey through life toward your heavenly city, where the blessed Virgin Mary intercedes as Mother and reigns as Queen.

We ask this through Christ our Lord. Amen.

Or:

Lord, in the blessed Virgin you have given your pilgrim Church an image of the glory to come.

May those who have fashioned this likeness of Mary look to her as a model of holiness for all your chosen people.

Grant this through Christ our Lord. Amen.

Bibliography

Bauer, Judith A., ed. *The Essential Catholic Prayer Book.* Liguori, MO: Liguori, 1999.
Callan, Charles J., and John A. McHugh. *Blessed Be God: A Complete Catholic Prayer Book.* New York: P.J. Kenedy, 1925.
Catechism of the Catholic Church. Washington, DC: United States Catholic Conference, 1994.
Lasance, F. X. *Emmanuel: A Book of Prayer.* New York: Benziger, 1953.
———. *My Prayer-Book.* New York: Benziger, 1908.
O'Day, Gail R., and David Peterson, eds. *The Access Bible: New Revised Standard Version with the Apocryphal/Deuterocanonical Books.* New York: Oxford, 1999.
"Order for the Blessing of an Image of the Blessed Virgin Mary" in *Book of Blessings.* New York: Catholic Publishing, 1989.
"Order of Crowning an Image of the Blessed Virgin Mary." Washington, DC: United States Catholic Conference, 1987.
Pelikan, Jaroslav, ed. *Sacred Writings, Volume 3, Islam: The Quran.* Translated by Ahmed Ali. New York: Book-of-the-Month Club, 1992.
The Roman Missal. Collegeville, MN: Liturgical, 2011.
Weller, Philip T. *The Roman Ritual, Volume II.* Milwaukee: Bruce, 1952.

www.ingramcontent.com/pod-product-compliance
Lightning Source LLC
Chambersburg PA
CBHW070102100426
42743CB00012B/2636